Vietnam War
Author: Perritano, John
Reading Level: 5.2
Points Value: 1.0
AR Quiz # 141276

959.7
PER

(

AMERICA AT WAR

VIETNAM WAR

JOHN PERRITANO

Library of Congress Cataloging-in-Publication Data

Perritano, John.

Vietnam War / [John Perritano].

p. cm. — (America at war)

Includes index.

ISBN-13: 978-0-531-23208-8 (hardcover)

ISBN-10: 0-531-23208-5 (hardcover)

1. Vietnam War, 1961-1975—United States—Juvenile literature. 2. United States—History--1961-1969—Juvenile literature. 3. United States—History—1969—Juvenile literature. I. Title.

DS558.P46 2010

959.704'3—dc22

2010035051

This edition published by
Scholastic Inc., 557 Broadway; New York, NY

SCHOLASTIC, FRANKLIN WATTS, and associated logos are trademarks and/or registered trademarks of Scholastic Inc.

269178 06/11

Printed in Heshan City, China
10 9 8 7 6 5 4 3 2

Created by Q2AMedia
www.q2amedia.com

Text, design & illustrations Copyright © Q2AMedia 2011

Editor Jessica Cohn
Publishing Director Chester Fisher
Client Service Manager Santosh Vasudevan
Art Director Joita Das

Senior Designer Rahul Dhiman
Project Manager Kunal Mehrotra
Art Editor Sujatha Menon
Picture Researcher Debobrata Sen

CONTENTS

POLISHED BLACK STONE

It was a crisp fall day in 1982. Thousands of military *veterans* met in Washington, D.C. The veterans gathered to *dedicate* the new Vietnam Veterans Memorial. This was no ordinary memorial. Vietnam had not been an ordinary war.

The Gathering

Many vets were in **combat fatigues**. Some came in wheelchairs or on crutches. About 58,000 names were on the monument's polished black stone. Each name stood for someone who had died in the war or was missing. Many of the former soldiers touched the names. Others wept. The memorial forced the nation to remember a war many wanted to forget. "It's like coming home," one vet said.

In the Beginning

Most U.S. troops sent to Vietnam served in the period from 1965 to 1971. They were fighting **communism**. Vietnam had been a French colony until World War II (1939–1945). Japan occupied the region during the war. France took control afterward. Then, communist leader Ho Chi Minh started a drive for independence. British, Chinese, French, Soviet, U.S., and other officials stepped in. The communists were given North Vietnam. Non-communists were placed in charge of South Vietnam. The North Vietnamese were not willing to accept the agreement, however. They decided to conquer the South.

Fighting Back

War between North Vietnam and South Vietnam broke out in 1954. The U.S. sent special troops to train South Vietnamese soldiers in 1961. The United States soon began supplying even more support to the South.

NORTH VIETNAM

CHINA

LAOS

THAILAND

CAMBODIA

SOUTH VIETNAM

Warring Nations:

North Vietnam, South Vietnam, United States

Leaders:

North Vietnam: Ho Chi Minh

South Vietnam: Ngo Dinh Diem
Nguyen Van Thieu

United States: John F. Kennedy, Lyndon Johnson, Richard Nixon

Top Generals:

General Vo Nguyen Giap: North Vietnam
General William Westmoreland: United States

Visitors to the memorial read the names of the dead and missing.

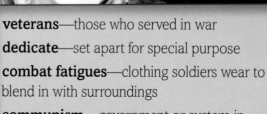

veterans—those who served in war

dedicate—set apart for special purpose

combat fatigues—clothing soldiers wear to blend in with surroundings

communism—government or system in which people have no property of their own

THE GULF OF TONKIN

U.S. officials feared what would happen if the communists took control of South Vietnam. Officials thought the neighboring nations would also fall. Those nations included Laos, Cambodia, Thailand, and Indonesia. The United States was not sure that South Vietnam could defend itself against the North. The North Vietnamese army was stronger.

First Shots

One of the early turning points of the fighting came on August 2, 1964. A U.S. Navy **destroyer** was patrolling the Gulf of Tonkin. That is a body of water off the coast of North Vietnam. North Vietnamese **torpedo** boats attacked the ship. Two more attacks were reported two days later. The August 4 reports were wrong. But by then it was too late.

President Johnson (far left) visits the U.S. and South Vietnamese military. ▼

Beginning in the Gulf

The U.S. took action on August 5. The U.S. president at the time was Lyndon Johnson. The U.S. Congress gave President Johnson permission to send troops to Vietnam. From that day on, the number of Americans in Vietnam grew. There were only 16,000 U.S. troops stationed in Vietnam in 1963. By the end of 1965, about 184,000 U.S. troops were "in country." That means they were stationed in Vietnam.

Many more thousands of U.S. troops would follow. Many thousands would die. Millions of Vietnamese on both sides would die.

Soldiers are decorated for bravery in battle.

Lyndon Johnson Acts

President Lyndon Johnson ordered the U.S. military to strike back against the North. He asked the U.S. Congress to give him the power to "take all necessary steps, including the use of armed force." Both the Senate and the House of Representatives thought it was the right thing to do. Most members of Congress were supportive of the president. Senator Wayne Morse of Oregon, on the other hand, called the move a "historic mistake."

destroyer—small, fast warship
torpedo—underwater bomb

ROLLING THUNDER

The war between the South and North heated up after the Gulf of Tonkin events. President Johnson thought that a mighty show of U.S. force would cause the communists to back down. Officials thought that U.S. support would allow South Vietnam to remain a separate nation.

Taking Charge

General Curtis E. LeMay was the U.S. Air Force's chief of staff. He favored air war and the use of bombs. LeMay said that U.S. bombs could send North Vietnam "back to the Stone Age." Johnson supported the idea of a bombing campaign. But he put limits on it.

First Combat Troops

The campaign was called Operation Rolling Thunder. It began in March 1965. U.S. bombers destroyed a weapons storage area. It was just north of the border between North and South Vietnam. The first wave of U.S. troops came ashore on March 8, 1965. The bombing campaign continued on and off for three years.

Rolling Thunder

Operation Rolling Thunder destroyed many bridges and other targets. More than a million pounds of bombs were dropped. The president and his **advisers** selected the targets to be bombed. Yet, the campaign was a failure. The North Vietnamese rebuilt whatever the bombs destroyed.

U.S. officials started with an air war.

advisers—those who give facts and their ideas

BATTLEFIELDS

Both sides got ready for ground war. The North had established several bases in the South. These bases included a key spot near the South China Sea. In August 1965, U.S. Marines began Operation Starlite. It was the first major military campaign of the war.

Operation Starlite

Marines landed at an area being held by the communist **guerillas**. The guerillas were called the **Viet Cong**. They had stationed thousands of soldiers at their base there. At first, the Viet Cong fought hard. Then they retreated. The Marines killed nearly 700 Viet Cong during six days of battle. The Viet Cong killed 45 Marines.

U.S. helicopters were called "horses." ▼

The Air Cavalry

The U.S. air **cavalry** was sent to the highlands of the South in October. Helicopters played an important role in Vietnam. These mechanical "horses" could carry troops into far-off areas. Helicopters could also fly at treetop level and fire at enemy troops. Helicopters **evacuated** the wounded from the battlefield.

The Chinook helicopter was made for heavy lifting.

The Battle of Ia Drang Valley

The North decided to attack in central South Vietnam. The North Vietnamese set their sights on Ia Drang Province. Winning there would split the country. This would give them an advantage. U.S. General William Westmoreland learned about the plan. He ordered the air cavalry into action. Colonel Harold G. Moore was the U.S. officer in charge. The North Vietnamese Army (NVA) attacked as Moore's troops were stepping off their helicopters on November 14. The fighting was hard and brutal.

The Americans called for help by radio. All available U.S. helicopters and airplanes came to the rescue. This airpower turned the tide of the battle. Moore's troops had stopped the NVA from taking over central Vietnam.

guerillas—those who conduct surprise attacks behind enemy lines

Viet Cong—communist guerillas in South Vietnam

cavalry—U.S. troops in Vietnam who used helicopters (named after troops who used to ride horses)

evacuated—cleared people out of an area

HO CHI MINH TRAIL

The communists could not match the Americans in firepower. Yet, the North could match wits. The communists built up the Ho Chi Minh Trail to become stronger. They used the trail to send supplies from North Vietnam to Viet Cong in the South.

The Ho Chi Minh Trail served as a ▼ supply route.

On the Trail

The Ho Chi Minh Trail was made of connected roads and paths. It had supply buildings and rest stops. The roadways cut through Laos and Cambodia. Those countries were not part of the fighting. They were **neutral**. The roads allowed the communists to attack nearly anywhere in the South. The trails covered 12,500 miles. Women and children carried rice and weapons along the Ho Chi Minh Trail. Boys on bikes also moved supplies. The Americans and South Vietnamese tried to stop the flow of supplies. Most attempts failed.

The DMZ

The five-mile-wide zone between North and South Vietnam was the **Demilitarized Zone (DMZ)**. The DMZ was supposed to be a border between the two countries. Yet, the North often crossed the DMZ to supply its troops. The U.S. wanted to stop the North's border crossings. They launched Operation Dye Marker. The U.S. plan was to build a wall along the DMZ.

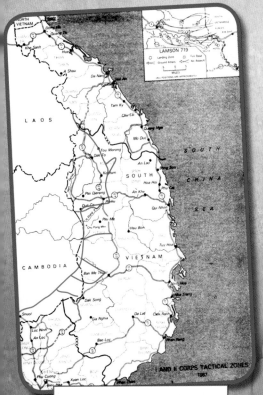

The Ho Chi Minh Trail (marked in red) was really many trails.

The wall had devices that sensed movement. The line had barbed wire, minefields, and watchtowers. The Americans never finished constructing it, however. Some of the war's heaviest fighting took place near the DMZ.

neutral—not taking sides in a conflict
Demilitarized Zone (DMZ)—enforced border

UNCONVENTIONAL WAR

World War I had its "doughboys." World War II had its "G.I. Joes." U.S. soldiers in Vietnam gave themselves the nickname "grunts." The name came from the sound the soldiers made while hauling heavy equipment on their backs.

New Realities

Many grunts thought the United States would win the war quickly. They were mistaken. Vietnam was a different kind of war. It was a young man's war. The average age of the U.S. soldier was just 19. World Wars I and II were fought by somewhat older soldiers. They used time-tested military **tactics**. In Vietnam there were no **front lines**. Instead, the enemy could be anywhere. Americans soon realized that old tactics would not work in the jungles of Vietnam.

The Americans realized that to win the war they would have to win the hearts and minds of the villagers. The U.S. military tried to win over the South Vietnamese. But many villagers simply supported whichever side left them alone.

Special Forces

The United States trained special groups of soldiers. They were taught about warfare in Southeast Asia. Among these groups were the Green Berets and Navy SEALs. These special soldiers gathered intelligence. They also directed gunfire and ran secret missions.

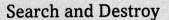

Search and Destroy

Most of the fighting in Vietnam took place between small groups of soldiers. Generally 40 or fewer fought most battles. American G.I.s would go out on "search and destroy" missions. They would march in hopes of finding and killing the enemy. But sometimes the jungle itself became an enemy. Soldiers often suffered from "jungle rot." That caused a horrible rash. The heat weakened the American troops. It was often hard for the Americans to tell who the enemy was. The NVA wore uniforms. Yet, the Viet Cong looked like regular people. Some Viet Cong were women and children. They would surprise American troops. The Viet Cong set **booby traps** for U.S. soldiers.

U.S. troops befriended villagers when possible.

tactics—science of arranging military forces to win

front lines—military positions in direct contact with an enemy

booby traps—hidden devices designed to harm an enemy

DATELINE VIETNAM

Many newspapers, magazines, and TV stations covered the war. Reporters and photographers came from all over. Historians often note, however, that Vietnam was the first televised war. Seeing images of war on television was new to people.

On the Story

Covering Vietnam was difficult. The **journalists** did not have computers, cell phones, or modern cameras. Instead, they filed their stories by telephone or by telegraph. Television crews carried big, heavy cameras. They filmed their reports and sent them to the networks. Americans watched the horrible battles each night on the news.

Americans watched war reports on television. ▼

Under Fire

Reporters often traveled with soldiers on missions. One of the most famous was Joe Galloway. Galloway served 16 months in Vietnam. He was the only reporter with Colonel Moore during the battle of Ia Drang. Galloway stayed on his stomach when the fighting broke out. He tried taking pictures without getting shot.

"I was down as flat as I could get when I felt the toe of a combat boot in my ribs," Galloway wrote about that day. An officer then told him to stand. "'You can't take no pictures laying down there on the ground, Sonny…' I thought: 'He's right.'"

War reporters like Joe Galloway became household names.

Galloway stood up and took pictures. He lived to tell the stories from that day.

Watching and Wondering

Television viewers who watched the Vietnam war reports began to question the war. Never before had the horrors of battle reached so far into American homes. TV viewers saw dead soldiers and villagers. Audiences were especially shocked after watching a famous story by CBS's Morley Safer. In Safer's report, U.S. Marines torched a village with cigarette lighters. These and other images affected public opinion in the United States.

journalists—those who report the news and try to find the truth

ANTI-WAR MOVEMENT

In the early 1960s, public support for the war was strong. But support for the war decreased. Americans began questioning the war. By 1968, many Americans wondered if it was time to bring the troops home.

In Protest

Groups of Americans spoke out in hopes of ending the war. The protesters included college students. Some young Americans fled to Canada. They did not want the government to **draft**, or force, them into the military.

Demonstrations

Thousands of protesters began holding antiwar **demonstrations**. One huge march on Washington, D.C., drew 500,000 people. Some members of Congress began questioning the war, too. Even some veterans coming home from Vietnam marched in protest.

Protesters often held "sit-ins." They would sit and not move. ▶

Joining Forces

Civil rights groups said the government needed to get out of Vietnam. They said we needed to help people at home. In 1967, Dr. Martin Luther King, Jr. said, "We have been repeatedly faced with the cruel irony of watching Negro and white boys on TV screens as they kill and die together for a nation that has been unable to seat them together in the same schools."

One of the most violent anti-war demonstrations happened during the 1968 Democratic Convention in Chicago. Police beat and arrested hundreds of protesters. The violence was seen on TV. The protesters shouted, "The whole world is watching!"

draft—send into service in the U.S. military; also known as *conscript*

demonstrations—shows of feeling made by groups with a message

19

THE TET OFFENSIVE

On January 31, 1968, millions of Americans watched the war news in horror. The U.S. Embassy in Saigon was under attack. The attack was the beginning of a major communist effort. General William Westmoreland was saying that the United States was winning the war. Now, many Americans were not so sure.

Breaking a Cease-Fire

The **offensive** took place during **Tet**. That is the new-year celebration in Vietnam. The holiday is the most important day on the Vietnamese calendar. Both sides agreed to stop fighting for three days. However, the communists used the cease-fire to make surprise attacks. The communists went after major cities and military bases throughout South Vietnam.

The Tet Offensive took place on the streets of Saigon and throughout South Vietnam.

News at the New Year

The short battle inside the U.S. Embassy in Saigon captured most of the world's attention. Viet Cong soldiers blew a hole in a wall and stormed inside. TV cameras were rolling. Americans killed the attacking Viet Cong. The firefight inside this seat of U.S. power shocked the world.

This fighting was part of the Tet Offensive.

Tet Offensive

The North thought they could get people in the South to rebel against their government. They wanted them to join the communist fight. The Viet Cong and NVA overran the city of Hue. They surrounded a U.S. Marine base. They targeted coastal cities that once had been safe from battle. The communists also went after U.S. headquarters. The Tet Offensive lasted nearly four weeks. It was a military failure for the North. The South Vietnamese did not rise up against the Americans. The North suffered heavy losses. Yet, the U.S. did not win, either. The fighting was fuel for the anti-war movement.

Four thousand U.S. troops died. So did 5,000 South Vietnamese. The images on TV angered many Americans. It looked as though the U.S. had lost the battle. American public support for the conflict dropped to a new low.

offensive—military plan of attack

Tet—new-year festivities in Vietnam, based on lunar calendar

W.C. Mills Elementary School
Wabash, IN

A CASUALTY OF WAR

The fighting in Vietnam harmed Lyndon Johnson's presidency. President Johnson wanted to fight a "War on Poverty" in the United States. He wanted to run a program he called the "Great Society." Yet, Johnson also did not want to lose in Vietnam. The cost of trying to do everything strained the U.S. government and funds.

Stalemate

By 1968, Vietnam had become a war of **attrition**. Each side tried to kill as many of the other side as possible. The president had promised Americans that the end of the war was in sight. He said there was a "light at the end of the tunnel." But Johnson and his advisers misunderstood the North Vietnamese. The North was willing to pay a huge price in human lives to win the war.

The number of U.S. ▶ troops in Vietnam reached a peak in 1968.

In the News

The press was reporting that Vietnam was a **stalemate**. Members of the press said the U.S. could not win. Even some of Johnson's advisers told the president that sending more troops would do no good.

President Johnson was in the White House from 1963 to 1968.

The Numbers

About a half million U.S. military people were in Vietnam at the end of 1968. The U.S. **economy** was in trouble. Anti-war demonstrations and riots in American cities added to Johnson's problems. He was up for re-election in 1968. Several politicians in his own party were running against him.

In March 1968, Johnson went on TV. He announced that he would cut down on the bombing of North Vietnam. He asked that peace talks begin. Then, the president stunned the nation. He said, "I shall not seek, and I will not accept, the nomination of my party for another term as your president."

attrition—the act of wearing down the opposing side by hurting soldiers

stalemate—deadlock; a situation in which further action is not possible

economy—ways of producing and distributing wealth

HAMBURGER HILL

Fighting decreased for a while after the Tet Offensive. The Viet Cong and the NVA were low on supplies. Then, the communists began stocking a major South Vietnamese base. The NVA wanted to use the South Vietnamese location for mission launches. It was near the DMZ. The United States and South Vietnamese decided to destroy the Viet Cong fort.

Apache Snow

Operation Apache Snow began on May 10, 1969. American troops took over a hill near the fort on the second day of battle. The North Vietnamese fought back hard. This was one of the worst battles of the war. U.S. troops called the battle a "meat grinder." History would call it "Hamburger Hill."

"Was It Worth It?"

A soldier wrote a letter home during the battle of Hamburger Hill: "I am writing this in a hurry. I see death coming up the hill."

Days of Death

The battle lasted nine bloody days. When the fighting was over, 630 communists were dead. Fifty-six Americans had died. Troops had to clear the hill of the dead. A U.S. soldier nailed a cardboard sign to a tree. It read, "HAMBURGER HILL." A second soldier added another sign: "Was it worth it?"

Americans had won the battle. But they soon abandoned the hill. The communists returned and took the area back a few days later.

WEAPONS OF WAR

The United States unleashed more firepower during the Vietnam War than in any war in history.

B-52 Stratofortress

One of the most deadly weapons was the high-flying bomber called the B-52 Stratofortress. The B-52s became the backbone of the U.S. air defense in Vietnam. These bombers were made to carry weapons over long distances. They were used to drop bombs from high in the air onto targets below.

Bombs drop from a B-52. ▲

Agent Orange

Fighting in the jungle was difficult. The United States used chemical sprays to destroy the jungle growth. That made it easier to see the enemy. Three of the most common mixtures were called Agent Orange, Agent White, and Agent Blue. The names came from the colors of the stripes on the big cans that held the chemicals. Most of the spraying was done with airplanes and helicopters. But sometimes soldiers did the work using spray that came from backpacks.

Pilots spray Agent Orange to destroy enemy cover.

Helicopters

The helicopter was used with success during the Korean War. But it was in Vietnam that the helicopter became very important. Helicopters gave U.S. forces more ways of getting around. Helicopters could take troops into a battlefield and then carry them out. The U.S. Army began moving huge numbers of troops into battle by air. Some combat operations used more than 100 helicopters at a time.

SAMs

The North Vietnamese used surface-to-air missiles that were built by the Soviets. The missiles were known as SAMs. The SAMs were deadly. They could find airplanes electronically. They could fly several times the speed of sound. They flew as high as 60,000 feet.

U.S. pilots had rules regarding SAMs. U.S. officials wanted to avoid killing people who were not soldiers. U.S. warplanes were allowed to bomb SAM storage sites only if they were at least at a distance of 30 miles from a city.

PRISONERS OF WAR

U.S. citizens were concerned about American prisoners of war. A treaty called the Geneva Convention had created rules of war. The rules included how to treat prisoners during wartime. Countries were not allowed to **torture**, kill, or shame prisoners of war (POWs).

Most POWs were pilots of downed aircraft.

No Protection

The POWs were protected by law. The North Vietnamese claimed that the rules did not apply to American POWs, however The U.S. Congress had not officially declared war before going into battle. The war was not official in this regard. U.S. soldiers were considered "pirates" by their enemies. The North treated U.S. prisoners as criminals instead of POWs.

The Hanoi Hilton

One of the most infamous prisoner-of-war camps in North Vietnam was Hoa Lo. The camp was also known as the "Hanoi Hilton." Hanoi was the capital of North Vietnam. Prisoners at the Hanoi Hilton stayed in their cells for long periods. They were tortured.

In January 1973, North and South Vietnam finally signed a treaty. The North released its American POWs. One of the first prisoners set free was Air Force Colonel Robinson Risner. He had spent seven and a half years at the Hanoi Hilton. President Richard Nixon asked to speak to the colonel over the phone. Risner took the call. He said, "This is Colonel Risner, sir, reporting for duty."

The "Hanoi Hilton" was first used to house political prisoners.

torture—to cause extreme pain

IN THE END

Richard Nixon had become U.S. president in 1968. Nixon was calling for "peace with honor." Most Americans did not support the war any longer. Yet, he expanded the fighting.

The U.S. conducted heavy bombings during Christmas of 1972. The next month, officials at last signed the "Agreement on Ending the War and Restoring Peace in Vietnam." The Americans had to leave in 60 days. The North had to release the POWs. Both North and South Vietnam broke the treaty, however. They battled for two more years. The Vietnam War did not actually end until the last U.S. troops left Saigon. The Americans cleared out in April 1975.

► A Marine helicopter lifts off from the U.S. Embassy in Saigon on April 30, 1975.

The **escalation** angered many Americans. Many protests broke out. A protest at Kent State University in Ohio was held in May 1970. National Guardsmen shot and killed several unarmed demonstrators. America seemed at war with itself.

Lessons of War

The effects of Vietnam can still be felt today. U.S. soldiers who returned to the United States after the war, felt unwelcomed. Some were even greeted by shouts of "baby killer" and "murderer." Many of the soldiers who had sprayed Agent Orange began suffering from cancer and other medical problems.

U.S. presidents since 1975 have tried to use the lessons of Vietnam. American leaders have tried to avoid wars that might drag on for years. Americans have tried to honor the soldiers who have served their country.

escalation—expansion of a conflict

Vietnam War Timeline

May 7, 1954
Vietnamese forces occupy the French fort at Dien Bien Phu

1961
President John F. Kennedy sends 3,000 military advisers to help South Vietnam in its war against the Viet Cong

January 12, 1962
U.S. helicopters fly South Vietnamese troops into battle. This marks the first U.S. combat mission against the Viet Cong

August 4, 1964
U.S. ships in the Gulf of Tonkin are said to be attacked. President Lyndon Johnson orders the U.S. to fight back

August 7, 1964
U.S. Congress passes the Gulf of Tonkin Resolution. This gives President Johnson the power to "defend" Southeast Asia

March 2, 1965
Operation Rolling Thunder begins

January 29, 1968
Tet Offensive begins

March 31, 1968
President Johnson announces he will not seek another term as president

January 27, 1973
A cease-fire agreement is signed by all warring parties

April 30, 1975
The last Marines guarding the U.S. Embassy leave South Vietnam

INDEX